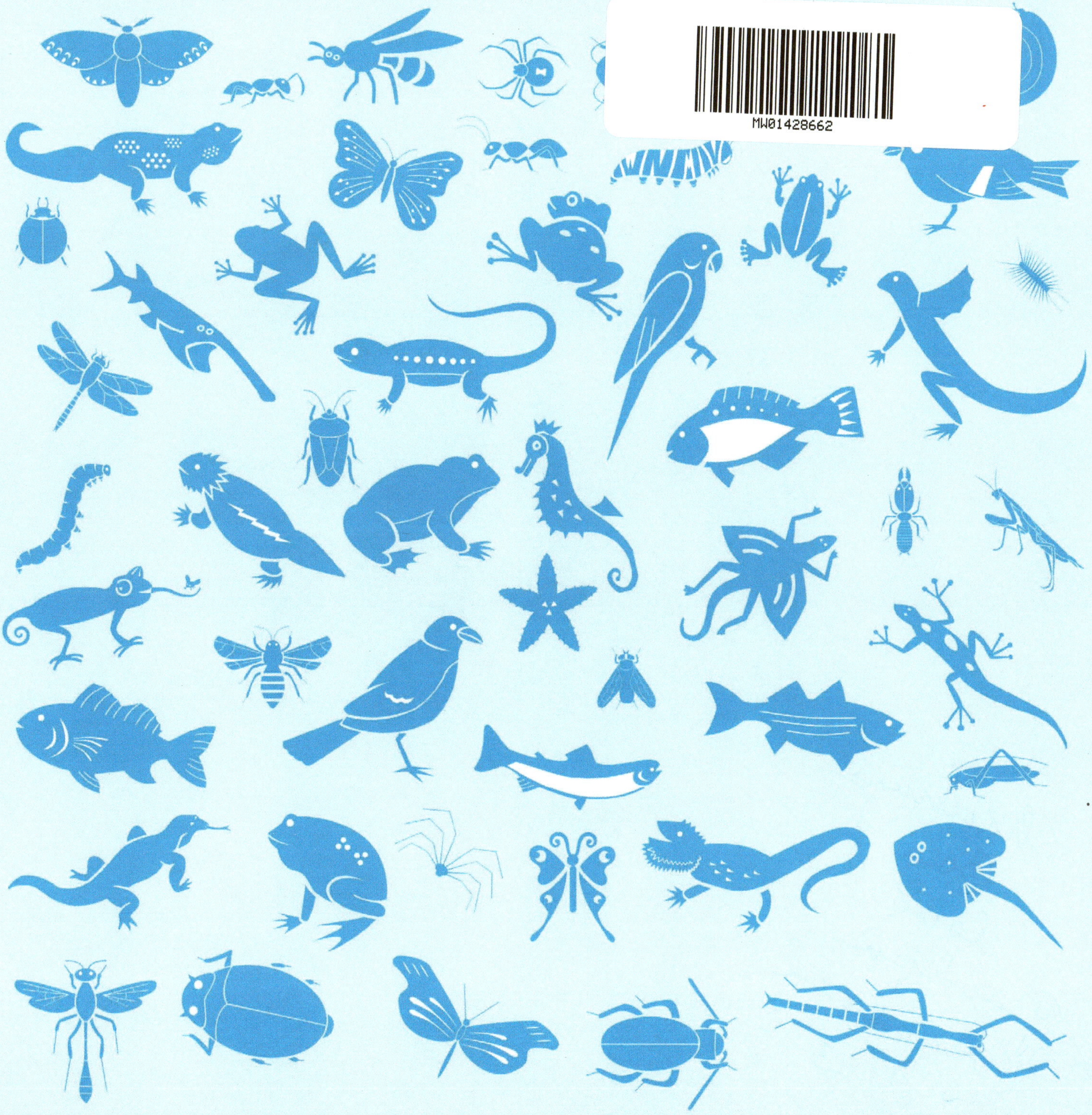

World of Bugs
Backyard Bugs

Bula Bug

Concept and Design by Brandee Hughes

Photography by Brandee Mae Hughes and Members of Placer Camera Club

Christmas Bugs! love grandpa grandma 2013

All rights reserved.

This book or parts thereof may not be reproduced in any form, stored in a retrieval system, or transmitted in any form by any means – electronic, mechanical, photocopy, recording, or otherwise – without prior written permission of the author, except as provided by United States of America copyright law.

DISCLAIMER : All insects, bugs, arachnids and the like are referred to as "bugs" in this book for simplicity. Children should not handle insects without adult supervision as some bugs can cause severe injuries, even death, if not handled properly.

Text & Design ©2011 Brandee Mae Hughes

Photographs by members of Placer Camera Club with the exception of page 7.

Edited by: Crystal Murphy

Published in the United States of America

ISBN -10 # 0-9838295-5-3

ISBN -13 # 978-0-9838295-5-3

For information on other books and products, please visit our website at

http://www.BulaBug.com or contact the author at brandee@bulabug.com

Follow us on twitter @BulaBugs or by visiting www.twitter.com/BulaBugs

Like us on Facebook at www.facebook.com/BulaBug

Photo Credits: Patrick Jewell -- front cover, back cover (fourth photo in line), 26, 27, 29, 42 (fourth photo in line); Fred Keillor -- back cover (first photo in line), 39; Jim Bennett -- back cover (second photo in line), 28, 42 (third photo in line); Mike Schumacher -- back cover (third photo in line), 7, 42 (second photo in line); Brandee Hughes -- title page, pg. 5, 6 (second photo in line), 8, 9, 11, 12, 13, 15, 17, 40; Janelle Bloomdale -- pg. 4, 16, 23, 24, 36, 37, 42 (first photo in line); Kristi Middleton -- pg. 6 (first photo in line); Karen Wyatt -- pg. 6 (third photo in line); Judy Hooper -- pg. 6 (fourth photo in line), 21; Tim Guthrie -- pg. 10; Nanette Means -- pg. 16; Bruce Gregory -- pg. 18, 19, 30, 32, 34, 35, 38, 41; Tony Hallas -- pg. 20, 31; Ardath Winterowd -- pg. 22; Carl Koening -- pg. 25, 33.

Contents:

Butterflies and Moths 3

Ladybugs 14

Bees and Wasps 18

Dragonflies 22

Praying Mantises 26

Spiders 30

Beetles 34

Flies 38

This book is dedicated to my Grandparents Shirley Mae Hughes and Robert Lee Hughes. You will always be with me.

A special thank you to my parents for always believing in me and supporting me in everything I do. Another thank you to Steve Outtrim for encouraging me to follow my dreams, and helping me make them a reality.

Bugs are all around us everywhere. They are crawling on the ground and plants, and flying through the air. Take a closer look and you will see, how amazing these little critters can be. Bugs are cute in their own unique ways. They like to come out to play on sunny days. Little bugs can crawl, swim, and fly. They come in all different colors, and some are quite shy. Bugs are the little creatures that do not get noticed much. So enjoy a closer look at this cute little bunch.

Butterflies and Moths

Image by Mike Schumacher

Image by Brandee Hughes

Butterflies and Moths start out as cute little caterpillars crawling around eating leaves. Once they get big enough, they go to sleep and turn into something else...

Image by Brandee Hughes

When the fuzzy little caterpillar is ready to sleep, it turns into a Chrysalis like this one. When the caterpillar wakes up, it will be a beautiful butterfly.

Image by Tim Guthrie

This beautiful butterfly has just emerged out of her chrysalis. Now she will soar through the sky looking for flowers where she will land to drink sweet nectar.

Image by Brandee Hughes

This little skipper butterfly has found a flower with sweet nectar inside and stopped for a drink. She drinks the nectar up with her long tongue.

Image by Brandee Hughes

Moths are different from butterflies because most moths fly at night and sleep during the day. Moths like this one sleep on windowsills during the daytime.

Image by Brandee Hughes

Moths like the bright lights in our homes at night and often fly in to get a closer look. This little moth found his way inside and is lounging on the couch.

Ladybugs

Image by Janelle Bloomdale

Image by Brandee Hughes

Bright red Ladybugs are hard to miss. They like to crawl around in gardens or on flowers and grass during sunny days.

11

Image by Nanette Means

Little Ladybugs like to gather in groups in the winter to stay warm. Then in spring they fly off to find sunny gardens and green grass. There they can munch on smaller plant eating bugs called aphids.

Image by Brandee Hughes

There are many different kinds of ladybugs. Some have spots and some do not, some are red and others are orange or yellow, and not all of them are ladies.

Bees and Wasps

Image by Bruce Gregory

Image by Bruce Gregory

Bees fly from flower to flower pollinating them to help make fruits and vegetables. Honey Bees also collect pollen and nectar that they make into yummy honey.

Image by Tony Hallas

Most Bees and Wasps build nests like this one. Some nests are for raising babies and some are for storing food. This baby wasp has just hatched.

Image by Judy Hooper

Honey Bees do a dance called the waggle dance when they return to their hive after searching for flowers. This dance tells other bees where to find the flowers.

Dragonflies

Image by Ardath Winterowd

Image by Janelle Bloomdale

Baby dragonflies are born in the water and live in the water their whole childhood until they become adult dragonflies. Then they come out of the water, shed their skin, and fly off into the sky.

Image by Janelle Bloomdale

As soon as they become flying adults, dragonflies soar through the sky in search of other bugs like mosquitos, flies, and bees to munch on. Once they find one, they snatch the bug right out of the air and eat it.

Image by Carl Koening

They can be found near water such as lakes and streams or flying through the sky in an open field. Dragonflies are among some of the fastest insects in the world and love to race from place to place.

Praying Mantises

Image by Patrick Jewell

Image by Patrick Jewell

Praying mantises eat other bugs. They are fast and strong and will snack on just about any bug they can catch.

Image by Jim Bennett

Praying mantises cannot fly when they are young, but grow wings as they become adults. Then they can fly through the sky.

Image by Patrick Jewell

Praying mantises are colored to blend in with the ground and plants around them. This camouflage helps them hide from lizards and birds that like to eat them.

Spiders

Image by Bruce Gregory

Image by Tony Hallas

Spiders can be all different colors, they can be smooth or hairy, round or pointy. There are many different varieties, but all spiders have 8 legs and most have 8 eyes too.

Image by Bruce Gregory

Spiders eat other bugs. Some spiders catch other bugs by hiding like this one and setting traps. Other spiders catch bugs in webs that they weave.

Image by Carl Koening

Some spiders like this black widow are very dangerous to humans. They have venom that they inject when biting. This venom paralyzes their food so that they can eat it.

Beetles

Image by Bruce Gregory

Image by Bruce Gregory

Beetles cannot see very well, so they use smells, sounds and vibrations to communicate with each other.

Image by Janelle Bloomdale

Beetles can be found almost everywhere in the world. They live on land and in fresh water.

Image by Janelle Bloomdale

Beetles eat all kinds of things including plants, pollen from flowers, seeds, other bugs, wood and fungi. Some beetles who live in the water even eat fish!

Flies

Image by Bruce Gregory

Image by Fred Keillor

Flies come in many different shapes and sizes. Not all flies are typical houseflies buzzing around the house like this one.

Image by Brandee Hughes

This harmless bee fly is mimicking a bee. Predators who want to eat the bee fly will leave it alone because it looks like a stinging bee.

Image by Bruce Gregory

Bugs are amazing and can do incredible things! Each of them are unique and beautiful in their own ways. Take a closer look and you will see, how incredible the *World of Bugs* can be!

"World of Bugs: Backyard Guide" the next book in the *World of Bugs* series, gets you face to face with the bugs in your backyard! Learn where to find them and how to catch them. Now you can safely & easily get a closer look at the bugs in your backyard!

Bula Bug would love to have your photos in our next book. Contact us today to find out more information about how to submit your photo in our World Wide Nature Photo Contest.

Enter your Nature Photo at
www.bulabug.com

Bula Bug
Nature Fun Store

Lots of great toys, kits and games can be found in our Nature Fun Store online. There are puzzles, books and live insect kits too! The Bula Bug Nature Fun Store has everything you need to have fun while learning about nature. Visit the store at BulaBug.com/store

The next book in the *World of* series is coming soon. Stay updated!

Like Bula Bug on Facebook

Follow Bula Bug on twitter

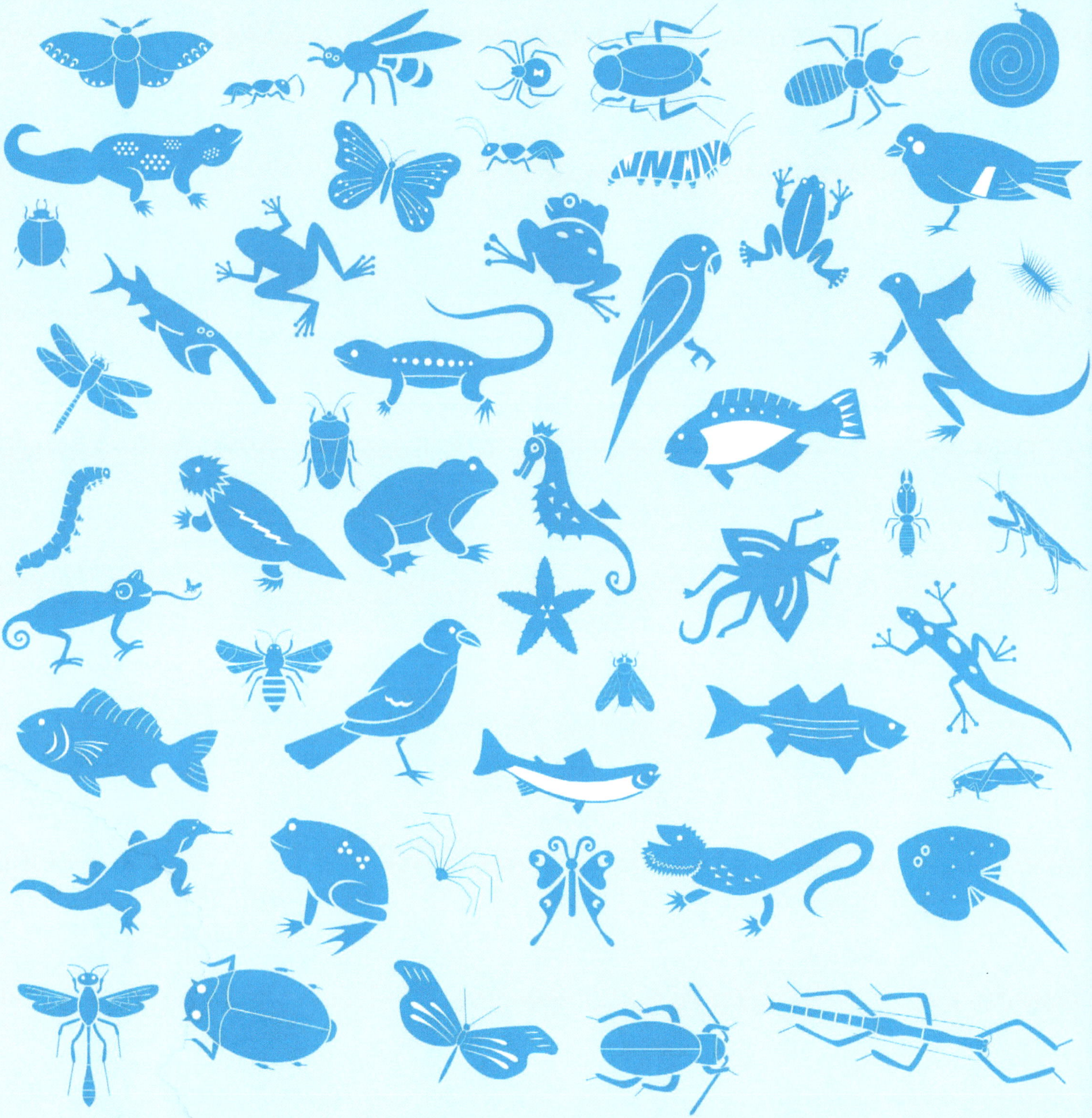

Made in the USA
San Bernardino, CA
02 July 2013